LIFE IN THE SHADOWS

Charleston, SC
www.PalmettoPublishing.com

Life In The Shadows
Copyright © 2023 by Diane Grossman Gaston

All rights reserved
No portion of this book may be reproduced, stored in a retrieval system, or transmitted in any form by any means–electronic, mechanical, photocopy, recording, or other–except for brief quotations in printed reviews, without prior permission of the author.

First Edition

Paperback ISBN: 979-8-8229-3100-8

Life in the Shadows

My Journey towards the sunlight

DIANE GROSSMAN GASTON

Contents

POEMS OF LONELINESS

PICKING UP THE PIECES..1
1982 – AGE 23

THE MIRROR OF TRUTH...2
1982 – AGE 23

FACE THE MUSIC..3
1979 – AGE 17

LOVE KNOWS THE WAY..4
1979 – AGE 19

ON THE INSIDE LOOKING OUT....................................5
1979 – AGE 20, (REVISED 1987, 2023)

WHERE IS THE LOVE?..6
1979 – AGE 20

MEN...7
1979 – AGE 20

PILLOW TALK 8
1979 – AGE 20

VISIONS OF LOVE..9
1980 – AGE 21

OUT OF TOUCH 10
1980 – AGE 21

WHAT'S WRONG WITH ME?.....................................11
1982 – AGE 23

THE PAINFUL SILENCE 13
1983 – AGE 24

PATIENCE 14
1983 – AGE 24

IF ONLY FOR ONE NIGHT...16
1983 – AGE 24

WHAT ISN'T THERE..18
1986 – AGE 27

OUT THERE SOMEWHERE.......................................19
1976 – AGE 17

LOVE AND ITS BURN..20
1987 – AGE 28

AS I REMEMBER LOVE 21
1987 – AGE 28

ABSENCE OF LOVE 22
1981 – AGE 22, (REVISED 1987)

DISAPPOINTMENT 23
1987 – AGE 28, (REVISED 1989)

LIFE IN THE SHADOWS 24
2023 – AGE 64

SECRETS 25
2023 – AGE 64

POEMS OF HOPELESSNESS

THE SAFE FLIGHT 29
1975 – AGE 16

HOW GREEN DIED TO MEET BLUE 30
1975 – AGE 16

FRAGMENTS 31
1986 – AGE 27

ETERNALLY THURSDAY 32
1987 – AGE 28

UP AGAINST THE GLASS 33
1986, 1987 –AGES 27, 28

NO WAY OUT 34
1986, 1987 – AGE 27, 28

THE INVISIBLE CHILD 36
1992 – AGE 33

THE INFERNO 38
1992 – AGE 33

THE JOURNEY HOME 39
1993 – AGE 34

THE TEARS I'VE CRIED 40
2007 – AGE 47

THE RAINBURST 42
2007, 2008 – AGES 47, 48

THE RAIN DANCER 44
1993 – AGE 34

TREADING WATER 45
2015 – AGE 46

HEARTBREAKER 46
1986 – AGE 27

WILL ONCE MORE EVER COME? 47
1987 – AGE 28

TRAPPED 49
1986 – AGE 27

THE FOG 50
1986 – AGE 27

THE BOOK OF DREAMS 51
1987 – AGE 28

DOWN FOR THE COUNT 52
1987 – AGE 28

SLIPPING AWAY 54
1987 – AGE 28

THE SEARCH 55
2007, 2008 – AGES 45, 46

POEMS OF LOVE LOST

THE DADDY WHO NEVER WAS 59
1975 – AGE 16

THE DADDY WHO NEVER WAS II 60
1979 – AGE 20

FANTASY FATHER 62
1979 – AGE 20

THE DRINKER 63
1987 – AGE 28

FATHER'S DAY 64
1988 – AGE 29

MISSING DADDY 66
1989 – AGE 30

THE DRINKER – THE FINAL CHAPTER 67
1996 – AGE 37

RUSTY DOG 68
1989 – AGE 30

BOB - WINGS IN HEAVEN 70
1979 – AGE 20

BOB – EXPLORING THE SKY 71

THE DECLINE OF DON

THE TREASURE..75
1989 – AGE 30

THE TRUTH...76
1991 – AGE 32

POTENTIAL...77
1991 – AGE 32

LETTING GO..78
1991 – AGE 32

BEGINNINGS AND ENDINGS..79
2007 – AGE 48

WHY I CRY...81
2008 – AGE 49

BROKEN PROMISES...83
2015 – AGE 56

POEMS OF SEARCHING

TAKING THE TIME TO FIND OUT*....................................87
1981 – AGE 21

THE STRUGGLE, THE SEARCH FOR ME.................................88
1987 – AGE 28

BEING ME..90
1988 – AGE 29

GROWING AWAY..91
1980 – AGE 21

AHEAD TO THE PAST...92
1987 – AGE 28

POEMS OF HEALING AND GROWTH

A FAMILIAR JOURNEY (FOR EILEEN).................................95
1979 – AGE 20

A WELCOME REST..96
1976 – AGE 16

BREAKING OUT..98
1979 – AGE 20

LOOK WHO I'VE FOUND...99
1980 – AGE 21

COMING UP FOR AIR..100
1983 – AGE 23

THE FIRST STEP 102
1983 – AGE 23

CATHARSIS 103
1986 – AGE 27

THE KEYHOLDER (FOR RICHARD) 104
1987 – AGE 28

A BREAK IN THE CLOUDS (FOR RICHARD) 105
1987 – AGE 28

WISDOM OF THE WAVES 107

WHAT'S MISSING 108
1987 – AGE 28

DIRECTIONS 109
1987 – AGE 28

OPENING UP 110
1987 – AGE 28

LIVING IN THE PAST 111
1987 – AGE 28

BEING THERE (FOR BRAD) 112
Introduced me to adult children of alcoholics meetings

THE MYSTERY TRIP 113
1988 – AGE 29

HEALING 114
1989 – AGE 30

SETTING LIMITS 115
1989 – AGE 30

THE CLEARING 116
1989 – AGE 30

CUTTING THE CORD 117
1980, 1987, 1989, – AGES 21, 27, 30

ONE DAY SOMEONE IS GOING TO HUG YOU SO TIGHT
THAT ALL OF YOUR BROKEN PIECES WILL STICK BACK
TOGETHER (FOR DAVID) 118
1987 – AGE 28

A HEALING TOUCH (FOR ANDY) 120
2023 – AGE 64

A HELPING HAND 121
1987 – AGE 28

Dedication

Originally, I hadn't really thought about a dedication page. It is mainly because I have had so many people who have inspired and motivated me. I am even including those people who caused my wounds, because if not for them, I wouldn't have put pen to paper to help survive all the challenges their wounds caused me to face. And of course, there are all the healing relationships that I managed to encounter, which provided support, and reassurance, that I was worthy of love. There were just too many people to narrow down a dedication. However, this changed on October 17th, 2023. As I was in the stages of marketing and formatting this book, I experienced the most profound loss of David, my best friend of the last 10 years, one of the healing relationships. He entered my life, at a real time of suffering, as I was facing the inevitability, and necessary transition of the ending of my marriage. He gave me the push that I needed to take this step. With him I discovered the validation, and worthiness, that had been deficits that were not only in my marriage, but that I experienced for most of my life. I told him once, "since I've known you, I like myself better." He said that was the best compliment he had ever received. He was ill before we met, so I prepared for his loss at the beginning of our friendship. For many years he fought, and waged temporary victories to stave off attempts for his body to take him down. He really got me. He wanted to get me. The second to the last poem is for him. My heart breaks for this loss. He didn't even know that I was publishing my poems, let alone, there being a poem for him. He said that he wouldn't have made it through his battles without me and thanked me for the times "that I talked him down from the ledge." Although I think he knew this, I want to thank him for saving me, and helping me to escape from my LIFE IN THE SHADOWS and for guiding me on MY JOURNEY TOWARDS THE SUNLIGHT.

Loneliness

PICKING UP THE PIECES

Please don't touch me, don't get too close,
Because I might feel something, and it will hurt,
Because the caress, ever so gentle, for only a short time,
Means love.
Then, when it's taken away, my heart goes with it, leaving a hole that never gets filled.
And just when I start feeling the hope sink in, I notice another hand trying to break through the wall to try and get me.
With suspicion, I look, but I don't budge.
Please don't touch me, don't like me, don't come near me.
I am alone and lonely, but I am safe from the pain that you will cause me.
I don't dare trust again.
I am scared, but I will die if I stay where I am.
What do I do?
Maybe I'm a fool, but I slowly reach out.
I cry because I know what will happen.
As the caress wakes me up and melts the ice.
I will be strong, as I take the hand.
The pain will hurt like hell when it's over.
But I've always survived before.
I often dream, imagine myself happy, even if it ends up,
To be only for a short time.
I decided that today's happiness is worth tomorrow's misery.
And I shall cling to it,
Because the caress, ever so gentle, for only a short time,
Means love.

THE MIRROR OF TRUTH

I looked into the mirror and saw reflections of the past.
I saw the things about myself that I hoped would never last.
That frightened little person who wouldn't face the world,
Finding growing up too hard, she stayed a little girl.

I looked into the mirror and saw reflections of the past.
Which made me think about myself, the time's gone by too fast.
How much I've changed, or so I thought, I still seem so much the same.
I do see scars of a long hard fight – a new me, except the name.

I looked into the mirror and saw reflections of the past.
As it seemed that all those things had finally left at last.
My life is not easy. It will never be.
But that mirror of my former self is still a part of me.

FACE THE MUSIC

The music was playing too loud.
I was very alone in the crowd.
I gave him a second chance,
But he still didn't want to dance.

He said that I stepped on his feet.
I said that he was always offbeat.
Then the record got stuck.
He said that I always brought him bad luck.

Pressure forced the needle to break.
One more scratch he just couldn't take.
After years the record has dust.
To hear it again is a must.

The music is playing too loud.
I am still alone in the crowd.

LOVE KNOWS THE WAY

My heart beats to keep me alive.
But it needs more than blood for me to survive.
My body is empty without love in its veins.
No love exists, so no life remains.

I am young, I don't want to die.
Love, please save me, please hear my cry.
The sound of a voice, the touch of a hand.
Why love hasn't yet found me, I don't understand.

The older I get, the stronger the pain.
Like the dying tree, the more it needs rain.
Warm my cold body, explore my bright mind.
Fill them with love, then life's what you'll find.

I am a beautiful person, when love's on my side.
I'm free from my shell, no more need to hide.
The more that you hold me, the longer I'll stay.
Love help me live, only you know the way.

ON THE INSIDE LOOKING OUT

Every night I stayed home alone, crying because I had no friends.
Just wondering if the loneliness was ever going to end.
I would listen to the radio, or I would watch T.V.
They were the only people who I would ever hear or see.

I could shut the power off, or I could turn the dial,
Until I found a sight or sound that I hoped would make me smile.
At school I was the nice girl, but I always had this doubt.
Everybody said they liked me, but I always was left out.

Gosh I hated school. I never went on dates.
I was back home with my T.V. that I would watch til very late.
But mostly I'd be crying because I had no friends,
Just wondering if this loneliness was ever going to end.

I guess I scared them off, but it was I who had the fear.
We just didn't understand each other, and backed off when we'd get near.
As I did get older, I tried hard to learn to trust.
For surviving in this lonely world, it really is a must.

But I'm afraid I'll still get hurt, even though I will survive.
I really hope that love will come and make me feel alive.
I still have nights I cry at home, hoping loneliness can end,
With the T.V. and the radio, as my only friends

WHERE IS THE LOVE?

I know there's nothing wrong with me,
Then why do I feel so bad?
The love and caring from one special guy,
Is something that I've never had.

Am I ugly or fat, is that why they don't call?
I can't quite figure it out.
I am such a nice girl with much love to give.
Tell me, what is it about?

Too many nights I sit home alone.
I cry, then I watch some T.V.
They say that they like me, but only as friends.
They don't notice the woman in me.

I get jealous and sad when I see others touch.
Why can't I be in those shoes?
I eat myself silly and get more depressed.
I am constantly having the blues.

Come get me Prince Charming and take me away.
Put some love in this cold empty heart.
One day I will find you and be saved by your love.
But until then my life cannot start.

I can love, I do love, I will love.
Please…give me a chance!

MEN

I've had it up to my ears with guys.
They're all alike. They all tell lies.
They say that they'll call you and you start to sing,
But that trusty old phone never does ring.

One day you'll meet one, and he'll say – "I really like you."
But before anything gets going, the relationship's through.
Without them you're lonely and you need them so bad,
But once you get them, they can make you so mad.

I tell you these guys, they're all the same.
They want only your body, and don't even notice your brain.
They hurt you so bad, that it makes you cry,
They call you a baby, with no understanding of why.

A girl is emotional, she tells what she feels.
A guy has to be tough, so he always conceals.
They'll break your heart, and then they'll find someone new,
While you're still picking up the pieces of what's left of you.

You hate them and love them at the very same time.
All of these guys, they're one of a kind.

PILLOW TALK

If pillows are meant to be slept on,
Then why are mine always so wet?
At night when I try to bring sleep to my eyes,
Teardrops are all that I get.

I feel so alone in my bed.
My body is so hard and so cold.
It needs to be touched, by someone's warm hand.
How I need somebody to hold.

I face each day with much pain.
And when I see other people in love,
My stomach starts hurting, my throat gets real tight.
I beg for help some help from above.

At these times when I get very low,
And feel that I haven't got worth,
I close myself in, and plan my escape,
From this great, lonely cruel planet Earth.

They tell me that I'll be okay,
And that things will soon be alright.
But I know the truth, it's plain as can be,
On my pillow night after night.

VISIONS OF LOVE

I think about the days ahead when I'll be with a man.
Our bodies being oh, so close, the touch of his warm hand.
His lips kissing every part of me, and still, I beg for more,
Causing sensations in my body, that I've never felt before.

The moment's drawing nearer for us to be as one.
I hope that I do please him. I hope we'll both have fun.
The air is thick with passion. Rhythm fills the night.
The sweat drips out of every pore, nothing ever felt so right.

The sleep is so fulfilling, but morning comes too fast.
Then I wake up and find myself alone, this is a dream that's just gone past.
I think about the days ahead when I'll be with a man.
So long I've waited, that I wonder if, I'm included in the plan.

OUT OF TOUCH

There are people all around me.
Then why do I feel alone?
So many faces of life going by.
It's their touch that I've not yet known.

Their arms swing aside them, helping them walk,
the link between brother and brother.
But most of the time, they're used as a shield,
To keep them from touching each other.

A hand in a hand, a face to a face.
A body dies without touch.
It goes to the heart, which pumps it with life.
A smile could mean very much.

There are people all around me.
They're so close, yet so far away.
Here are my hands, they are reaching out,
For a chance to live one more day.

WHAT'S WRONG WITH ME?

She pressed her face against the window causing a fog that she had to wipe away with her hand.

The other kids were playing tag across the street, laughing, screaming and just having fun.

She tried, with all of her strength, to keep from crying, but her eyes welled up with tears and a drop rolled down her cheek, and gently landed on her sleeve.

The cat came up to her and started rubbing against her leg, and with one swift motion, she scooped it up in her arms and hugged it ever so tight… The only true friend in her world.

She tried to play with, and make friends with the other kids, but after awhile they would ignore her.

They would play tricks on her and hid from her whenever she came by. Kids can be so cruel.

The jolly jingle of the ice cream truck filled the air with delight.

Everybody went racing towards the sound.

One by one each kid ordered his treat. When the last person finished, she got up and took change from the dish that sat on the desk by the door, and walked out toward the truck where the man was just getting ready to move on.

She ordered a cherry popsicle and an Eskimo Pie.

She attacked the desserts as if they would disappear into thin air.

Half-way through her second snack, she heard a snickering from behind the neighbor's bush that divided their houses.

The little face of the boy next door popped out.

He was laughing hysterically at and pointing at her and the sticky mess all over.

She ran upstairs to her room and slammed her door behind her.

She flung herself on the bed and cried hysterically into her pillow.

She propped herself up, looked outside and saw the little boy run back across the street.

She turned on the T.V. and stared blankly at the screen.

The cat, who had found his way in, jumped on the bed and curled up at her feet.

THE PAINFUL SILENCE

Throughout my life I've had much pain
From those who never called again
The time we'd spend was never long.
When I'd start to feel they would then be gone.

They were never love; they didn't have long enough chances.
They were only sweet, but very short romances.
So many times, my heart was torn in two,
Too badly broken to be mended by glue.

So, every time I feel the touch of love,
I shy away and put on a glove.
I know I'll get hurt, so why even dare?
They're all alike. None of them care.

But each person is different. I have to be fair.
Maybe he has something different that he wants to share.
I am going to have to learn how to trust.
To live a full life, it's a definite must.

I am really scared. I don't want the pain,
Of one more man who won't call me again.
I have to risk, or I will never grow.
If I don't take the chance I never will know.

PATIENCE

I want to be loved. Is that too much to ask?
It seems to keep passing me by.
I just get so close. Tell me, what do I do?
They fade away and I start to cry.

I want a man to hold me so close.
A basic need, the need to be touched.
I long for the day when I'll finally hear,
"Darling, I love you so much."

What am I doing? Why is it so hard,
For love to find me and stay.
I've had so much pain. It just isn't fair.
This sadness just won't go away.

Too many times, tears fill my eyes.
Laughter rarely is heard.
Sometimes I want to run away from it all,
And wish for wings to fly like a bird.

He wakes up my body, he warms up my heart.
Then he leaves as quick as he came.
He gave me hope. It lasted not long.
Now things are just not the same.

I want love so bad. I've waited so long.
I'm tired of being alone.
I see myself older, and still without love.
I want somebody who will be my own.

When the pain gets real bad, I sometimes will say,
That it would be better if I ended it all.
I'd be at peace. The hurt would be gone.
No more picking up after the fall.

Deep down inside, I don't want to die.
Somewhere there's a love just for me.
I must open my heart, my soul, as well as my eyes,
Before I am able to see.

I won't give up on love. It will come in time.
It will find its way to my door.
All the time that it's taking to find the right path,
I figure it's worth waiting for.

IF ONLY FOR ONE NIGHT

Take hold of my hand, if only for one night.
Hold on to my body, so very, very tight.
Tell me that you'll want me, that you'll love me for this time.
Even though it won't last long, for a moment you'll be mine.

Kiss my entire being. Melt my cold, cold heart.
Make that sweet, sweet love to me to every single part.
I need to feel I'm pretty. Your touch will tell me so.
I want to hear that I'm alright. I really need to know.

Should I take the chance of getting close too fast,
Knowing that right from the start that it isn't going to last?
Love has not been very kind. It never stays too long.
But I know that just because it's short doesn't have to mean it's wrong.

Right now, I'm feeling pain of a love that's gotten lost.
I made a very big mistake and I'm suffering the cost.
I'll think in simple terms. I'm trying to learn how,
To take the love that comes my way, because it's more than I have now.

The offer is so tempting. I know I'll feel so good.
But knowing of the next day's pain, I don't know if I should.
I am so very lonely. I so much need someone near.
To let me know that I'm a woman and to wipe away my tears.

I know that you will give me all the love you can.
All the love my body needs that can come only from a man.
I'm holding out my hand to you if only for one night.
Because anything that eases pain is a thing that must be right.

WHAT ISN'T THERE

The loudest sound that I can hear,
Is the sound of nothing in my ear.
No ringing of the telephone, no knocking at the door.
Just echoes of a silence that lets go its mighty roar.

The saddest letter that I can get,
Is the one I haven't gotten yet.
No writing of a note, or a card to say hello.
Just shadows of a vision, that fail to make a show.

The most painful feeling I'll ever feel,
Is the lack of love from someone real.
No touching of a heart, no holding of a hand.
Just wishes of a beauty that I want to understand.

OUT THERE SOMEWHERE

I looked at me and all that I could see was a person without love.
A woman alone, with no man of her own – a body without touch.

Going nowhere, longing for somewhere.
Needing direction, in search of perfection.
Afraid of rejection, but still needs protection.
I'll go anywhere with someone who'll care.

I looked around and heard not a sound, except the beat of a lonely heart.
I am a woman who knows that it's with love that I'll grow in body and in mind.

Aching for anyone but wanting the right one.
Needing affection, there's such a selection.
For fear of infection, they must pass inspection.
I'll stay with someone, somewhere, sometime soon.

I looked behind and was surprised to find that I am not unique.
A woman alone, who was now being shown, that she should not feel ashamed.

I'm part of the everybody, who's looking for somebody.
Being in the collection, in search of perfection.
Still needing protection but fearing rejection.
We will go anywhere with someone who cares.

I looked ahead, there's no more to be said, I must stop being scared.
I'm a woman who knows that with patience I'll grow, and when love finally does show, I will then know that it was worth waiting for.

LOVE AND ITS BURN

I feel an emptiness deep down inside.
It's the absence of love; it has finally died.
I would give, and I'd give, but would never receive.
With its energy wasted, it decided to leave.

This heart took a beating, til it was battered and bruised.
Hoping for just one winner, each time it would lose.
Good times appeared, I again played the fool,
For I soon would be crying. Love can be so cruel.

So many promises made in the dark of the night,
Were promises broken when the dark turned to light.
Time and again tears filled my eyes.
From feeling so hurt by all of the lies.

I ended the battle. The war had been won.
As I shut myself off until I was numb.
The brief moments of good are not worth all the pain.
So, this decision to not feel again.

This emptiness that is deep down inside,
It may never be filled for I do have my pride.
I have given my all just to get in return,
The pain of the flame of love, and its burn.

AS I REMEMBER LOVE

It's been a while, since I have smiled, or felt a touch.

I close my eyes and begin to cry, as I remember love.

The tears roll down my cheek. I feel a little weak.

Being close, feeling warmth, kissing, hugging.

It's all just a memory.

I open my eyes, I can't stop the cries, for I am all alone.

Remembering the past – the pain.

Living in the present – the pain.

Hoping for the future – the pain?

It's been a while, try and make me smile.

I am tired of all the tears.

For I close my eyes, and each time I cry. I feel a little weak, and the drops roll down my cheek.

It's been a while, since I have smiled, or felt a touch.

I miss it so much.

As I remember love.

ABSENCE OF LOVE

I feel the pain of years without love:

I miss all the times when one tender kiss would have made everything be alright.

And all of the days when I felt so alone and ached for loving all through the night.

Just being held when I was so low would have helped to ease all my fears.

And the touch of a hand, so gentle and warm, could have wiped away all my tears.

I've never heard the phrase "I love you:"

The eternal absence of these three little words has created quite a large hole.

The longer it's missing, the more that it burns much deeper into my soul.

Please hear my cries, I really need help. I'm slipping back into my shell.

Take hold of my hand, I need to be saved, from this painful and so lonely hell.

DISAPPOINTMENT

He said that he would call, but still, I hear no sound.
As each day goes by, the more I am let down.
Now I start to cry. The sting it is so real,
As I try and blink away the disappointment that I feel.

The silence roars so loud. I put my hands up to my ears.
Getting louder every moment that the sound does not appear.
I thought that we were friends, but now I have this doubt.
As I wait and wonder what friendship's all about.

Time and time again the phone just does not ring.
So much hurt and heartache this machine does bring.
There are still so many tears, the sting's so very real.
As I try and blink away the disappointment that I feel.

LIFE IN THE SHADOWS

All my life I have lived in the shadows,
Where I've been alone for so many years,
And where no one ever does notice,
That I am crying an ocean of tears.

Sometimes I look out the window,
And watch the birds in the sky up above,
Then I feel this ache in my heart,
From what's missing – it's the absence of love.

I'm so tired of being this sad girl,
From wanting what I just can't have.
I find myself always getting lost,
When I try searching for the right path.

At times I just don't understand,
And ask God – "Why is it this way,
Having to work so very hard,
At only surviving day after day?"

I've felt so lonely having lived in the shadows.
It was my life for so many years.
And when someone finally does notice,
I will have already drowned in my ocean of tears.

SECRETS

I live my life holding so many secrets,
That I keep safely locked deep inside.
And as long as I don't tell you my secrets,
All my pain I will continue to hide.

It's way too risky to tell you,
Because I know that I'll start to cry.
So even when you do ask me,
The only choice I can make is to lie.

I don't know if I really can trust you,
To understand how I truly do feel.
And even when you look into my eyes,
These secrets I still won't reveal.

For I'm afraid that you'll no longer love me,
With the truth hidden deep in my soul.
For I'll be shattered into millions of pieces,
And I never again will be whole.

I don't want you to feel sorry for me,
So, all my pain I will continue to hide.
I might be alone, but I'll still have my secrets,
That I keep safely locked deep inside.

HOPELESSNESS

THE SAFE FLIGHT

Outside there are people singing.
To each other they are clinging.
Joy and laughter they are bringing.
Outside there are people singing.

All these hearts are filled with love.
Peace, they bring us from the dove.
Sounds like angels from above.
All these hearts are filled with love.

Join them in their merry song,
For they are doing nothing wrong.
Raise your voices loud and long.
Join them in their merry song.

The happy tunes are heard no more.
Instead, we hear the sounds of war.
In the sky the bird does soar.
The happy tunes are heard no more.

HOW GREEN DIED TO MEET BLUE

The seed is planted.
It will grow high.
If the sun shines too strong,
It soon will be dry.

With too much water,
The roots will be drowned.
With the force of the wind,
It'll soon be knocked down.

The seed is planted.
It will grow high.
Without proper care,
The whole thing will die.

The small seed is stepped on.
Nothing remains.
It its short life,
It knew only pain.

The seed is planted,
It can no longer grow high.
Without help of man,
It would have seen sky.

FRAGMENTS

Right now, I'm so tired, I feel weighed down.
Get your hands off my shoulders, I am starting to drown.
Buried under the pressure, help me find a way out.
I push and I shove, "I give up!" I do shout.

So long I've been climbing this eternal ladder,
Getting closer to nowhere, getting madder and madder.
I want to jump off, and give up the fight,
But it's so dark at the bottom, and up ahead there is light.

ETERNALLY THURSDAY

It always seems to be Thursday,
As the weeks quickly pass by.
I ask – "Where does the time go?"
As I look out the window,
And I let all the tears flow.
I feel as grey as the sky.

The clouds are promising rain.
And life keeps giving me pain.
Hopes rise only to fall.
I am so tired of it all.
Oops! One more wall.
The same old story again, and again.

I am becoming boxed in.
As another week is nearing the end.
The past makes me so mad.
The future seems not to be had.
Right now, I'm so sad.
When will I be on the mend?

It always seems to be Thursday.
Time passes with the blink of an eye.
Each day seems the same.
They go as quick as they came.
Another week of blues, and no fame.
I look outside and I let myself cry.

UP AGAINST THE GLASS

I am so shy,
So often I cry.
I lock myself in.

Away from the pain,
Safe from the rain.
I am dry and alone.

Afraid of them all.
So sure I will fall.
Then they will laugh.

I scream and I shout.
I so much want out,
But so often I fail.

Why can't they see,
That I want to be free?
I do need them so.

But I don't believe,
I just can't conceive,
That I have any worth.

When will someone take my hand?
I just can't understand...
Damn! I do deserve love.

NO WAY OUT

My car, I drove it home,
To a place where I had grown.
Not so very many miles
To relive the tears and smiles.

I close my eyes and feel.
The pain that was so real
I remember all those years,
I was so full of many fears.

My room, it was my shell.
A private little hell.
The only place I knew,
Where pain could not break through.

I found ways to cope.
I never gave up hope.
I wrote to keep me sane.
I ate to ease the pain.

When I moved away,
I thought I'd be okay.
But even though the place had changed.
I still did feel quite strange.

My room again was hell.
I was back inside my shell.
As I wrote to keep me sane,
And ate to ease the pain.

No matter where I drive my car,
It isn't very far,
For whether there or here,
I live the smiles and tears.

THE INVISIBLE CHILD

This little child sits alone. There is nowhere she can turn.
This loneliness is like a fire. The more it grows the more it burns.
She has a face that disappears when she's amongst a crowd.
She has a voice that no one hears even when she cries out loud.

She looks in the mirror and wonders why she ever had been born.
But life and death can both cause pain; with this decision she is torn.
She hates the world, she hates herself. She finally gives up hope.
All life from her is slowly drained. She has no energy to cope.

No one holds her. No one cares. No one ever sees her pain.
No one notices how hard she fights in her struggle to keep sane.
She's just a child, yet she's already learned harsh lessons on this earth.
That somehow, she does not count and that she has very little worth.

Although she's here because of love, it's something she's never known.
The people who just gave her life have since left her all alone.
She rolls herself into a ball, and crawls into her shell.
It's the only way that she has found to escape this life of hell.

She has a broken heart and a wounded soul. She has cried up all her tears.
They all went to waste on her pillowcase, which has been soaked for many years.
She is a precious gift that has been tossed aside, as she is locked up in her room,
Where she spends her days as the clock ticks off an eternity of gloom.

The flames are causing many burns as they continue growing higher.
With nowhere to turn she finds herself being swallowed by the fire.
Her face has forever disappeared. Her voice no longer cries out loud.
Her loneliness is finally gone, as she waves goodbye to the crowd.

THE INFERNO

My fear is like a raging fire that burns without control.
It consumes whatever's in its path and is swallowing me whole.
My heart pounds and pounds a rapid beat deep inside my chest.
The rhythm invades my very soul and does not let me rest.

When I sleep the dreams inside my head remind me of my fright.
Vivid pictures of this girl in pain awaken me at night.
It's like I'm falling without a net, and I cannot see below.
It hurts me so to reach for help. I'm too scared to let them know.

I feel the tears of all this pain bubbling deep inside.
It's so hard for me to let them out, but so much they must be cried.
My fear is like a raging fire that burns inside my soul.
I hope there's magic in those gentle drops that will help to make me whole.

THE JOURNEY HOME

I've spent so many years just trying to fight through all the pain.
I work so hard to find the sun only to get soaked by all the rain.
I have this fear that I will slowly sink into the ground.
And on this trip the seas will flood and helplessly I'll drown.

All this pain is caused by what I've lost and never had.
I can't let it go, so instead I choose to let it keep me sad.
All this rain is my own tears that have settled in my heart.
Which gets so full, it skips a beat so my life just will not start.

A rainbow is a fantasy of a beauty I cannot see.
Colors beyond black and grey are just never meant to be.
There's this endless storm that rages on and forever fills the skies.
It's equal to the tears not shed which puts pressure on my eyes.

I don't know how much longer I can fight through all this pain,
And keep my head above the flood, and not drown from all the rain.
For certainly I will slowly sink into the ground.
It will be the fear of my own tears that in the end will bring me down.

THE TEARS I'VE CRIED

I close my eyes and feel,
This pain that is so real.
And when I open them real wide,
You might see the tears I've cried.

Each beat of my heart,
Tears me more and more apart.
Instead of keeping me alive,
I am fighting to survive.

I feel wounded in my soul.
I no longer feel whole.
The mirror I was shown,
Showed me how little I have grown.

The flaws that make up me,
I have failed to really see.
And these errors that I've made,
Are now leaving me afraid.

I allow time to pass me by.
How much harder I must try,
To move on with my life,
As a woman, mother – wife?

Because the pain that I do feel,
Is so very, very real.
And when I open my eyes wide,
You will see the tears I've cried.

THE RAINBURST

My days blend together as if they were one,
With very few moments where I feel the sun.
I'm in a shell I can't open, as I work hard to pry,
With much pain of defeat, I then start to cry.

Wherever I turn, the path is the same,
As it heads me to nowhere, so who do I blame?
When I look in the mirror, I see a sad me.
I'm afraid to speak up to help to get free.

I'm tired, so tired from being put to the test,
Of working my heart out without any rest.
I'd like to run far away to where now's out of view,
To find a safe place to begin things anew.

But there's so much burden as I sort through my life.
I'm the mother of children, and for now, I'm a wife.
What do I keep, and what do I let go,
So, at last I can breathe and finally grow?

So rarely I watch the sun setting at night.
I stay inside my shell and fight the good fight.
Each day's like slow motion, yet time passes fast.
I'm spinning my wheels – how long can this last?

"What do I want?" I keep asking myself,
As I am gradually losing my mental health.
For my head keeps on spinning in dark clouds of grief,
Awaiting the rainburst to bring me relief.

My anger is old being built on for years,
But I'm ready for changes despite all my fears.
Action is vital, my heart and soul are at stake.
Choices need to be made, as there are risks I must take.

I want my days to be separate to live one by one,
Where I'm nourished to grow by the warmth of sun.
I'm working hard to pry myself out of my shell.
I can't stay defeated – may my tears release me from hell.

THE RAIN DANCER

All my tears hide behind my eyes with this fear that they might fall.
The secret will at last be out; my pain will be seen by all.
You now will know just how much I really hurt inside.
You now will know how much pain I'm in as you see the tears I've cried.

My heavy heart, it weighs me down with the pain from all I've lost.
People and things I can't replace; my soul is what it has cost.
There is this picture in my mind of this girl who isn't me.
A happy girl so full of life is a dream that just can't be.

Like my life, the rain falls hard, and like my life the wind blows strong.
The worst of the storm has come my way, I just hope it won't last long.
There is this hole I cannot fill. There is an echo from within.
That is calling out for someone's help, because alone I cannot win.

My tears are getting very tired, knowing soon they will have to fall,
And take the risk of coming out and being seen by all.
You cannot help me with my pain unless you see the tears I've cried.
And then at last you will finally know how much I really hurt inside.

TREADING WATER

It seems wherever I turn, I feel sad and let down,
In a sea of tears I have cried, I fear soon I will drown.
With no one left to save me to hold out a hand,
To help guide me safely back to dry land.

There were people whom I thought I could trust.
But right now, it feels like I've been left in the dust.
It's hard to think, that although once they did care,
That now when I need them, they just aren't there.

Maybe I'm the reason that they disappear,
What else could it be as to why they're not here?
Do I just attract others who end up leaving?
As it seems I'm always in the process of grieving.

I've been in the background for most of my life,
In school, as a daughter, a sister – a wife.
Starved for attention, I was lost in the crowd.
I never was heard, despite my crying out loud.

As I barely tread water, trying hard not to drown,
In the sea of tears, I have cried from being let down.
With all of my strength I will reach out my hand,
In hopes I'll safely be guided back to dry land.

HEARTBREAKER

He looks at me and smiles and asks me for my name.
It gets my heart to racing, I hesitate just the same.
Just another talker who's out to tease my heart.
False hopes he's good at selling; his perfected art.

There out to be a law against these types of men.
They get away with murder, time and time again.
I get tired of that old promise – "I'll give you a call."
If they never meant to do it, it should never have been said at all.

WILL ONCE MORE EVER COME?

Will there be a once more for us to be as one,
And to share the heat of passion where we'll both have fun?
It hasn't been that long since we have been friends.
So soon that we were lovers. I am fearful of the end.

Will there be a once more? I hope and wait and pray.
For I don't know what you're thinking, and dread what you might say.
Were we just caught up in the moment, or was this the start?
Should I look forward to more pleasure, or the breaking of my heart?

Will there be a once more? Oh, how I want it so.
For you were so gentle, and there's so much more I want to know.
I don't know when I'll see you, or if you'll ever call again.
Will we have a good time, or will it be a strain?

Will there be a once more? So hard I fight the tears.
Remembering our first time. Is there cause for all my fears?
It was something that I dreamed of, and never thought would be.
I just could not believe that you also wanted me.

Will there be a once more where we will be as one,
Sharing all that passion, and having all that fun?
So soon that we were lovers. So short to be just friends.
So fearful of the pain that might lead to our end.

Will there be a once more? All these knots I can't break free.
You tied them all so tight when you made love to me.
In the fit of passion, so many things were said.
But how many will stay true after we are out of bed?

Will there be a once more? I am so much confused.
Did this all mean something, or am I being used.
My dear sweet tender friend, with all the gentleness you bring.
My heart will now break slowly for the phone that doesn't ring.

TRAPPED

Sometimes I feel like I'm in a box. To be heard I have to shout.
I can look and see the other side. No one hears to let me out.
Every time I think I have found the right path, I run into a wall.
And every time that I take a step, I always trip and fall.

I am losing touch with who I am. I only know my name.
I can't hold on to any goal. I have only myself to blame.
I knock on doors, and they let me in. They seem a friendly place.
But, by the time I turn around again, they're slammed back in my face.

Bouncing back is hard, when all the walls are made of stone.
Crawling on my hands and knees; when I stand up, I'm standing alone.
I go back to my corner for a bit of peace, weary from the fight.
I try to rest, but instead I cry. Hope seems to be out of sight.

Right now, I feel like I'm in my box. I'm screaming to be let out.
I am trying to reach the outside world. I can see it without a doubt.
I will try and take another step, holding on so I won't fall.
Here I go again, still wondering if, I'll ever make it there at all.

THE FOG

I looked out the window and started to cry,
Despite the beauty and warmth in the sky.
I feel as empty, my mood is as blue,
As tears cloud my vision and spoil the view.

I look at the present: reflect on the past.
But I see the same picture…a long time it can last.
All of the tears and the rain didn't wash it away,
Though the color is quite faded with replacements of grey.

The sun goes on shining so big and so bright.
But my days remain cloudy, and then dark of night.
My heart aches for something the sky can't fulfill.
A sight or a sound. I'm not quite sure still.

I stare out the window and continue to cry.
With all of this beauty, I don't understand why.
I am getting so tired; my mood is still blue.
Weary eyes cloud my vision, then they close, no more view.

THE BOOK OF DREAMS

See the little girl at school sitting all alone.
Crying silent tears, she has no friends to call her own.
Time keeps slipping by her, as there goes yet another day,
That she looks with longing eyes at the other kids at play.

On the bus ride home she's as quiet as a mouse.
Then the driver honks his horn, she runs the 3 blocks to her house.
Safely in her room making sure to lock the door,
She lets go of the tears she can't keep silent anymore.

No one ever visits her, no one ever calls.
She keeps herself a prisoner behind that door and its four walls.
She writes inside her journal and tells it of her pain.
It's the only one she talks to in her struggle to keep sane.

She writes to God and begs him for things to be okay,
And that she's tired of being lonely and crying every day.
I don't think he's really up there. If he is he's not that smart,
For he's letting her die slowly by the breaking of her heart.

DOWN FOR THE COUNT

It's been a long, long time since I have felt alive.
As each day goes by, I manage only to survive.
Happiness and pleasure have failed to appear.
Heartbreak seems to manage to linger ever near.

Each day the sun does shine, as I wake up in a rage,
As the cloud that hovers over, surrounds me like a cage.
I am always on the inside fighting to get free.
A forever endless nightmare is this struggle to be me.

Time just beats me up as I receive yet another blow.
All these shots of pain – are they supposed to help me grow?
I am hurting and I'm tired, as the bell rings for one more round.
I continue with the battle – again I get knocked down.

When will someone notice that I've more than paid my dues,
And reward me with some pleasure, and take away the blues?
Life is more than just surviving, and heartbreaks every day.
Happiness is owed to me, just let it find the way.

HOLDING ON

Sometimes I wish it were always today.
Tomorrow brings pain that won't go away.
Today I am safe. I still am alive.
When the next day comes, I may not survive.

Yesterday was such a terrible time.
The world fell apart, no friends could I find.
I am so lonely; I need to be saved.
I so much need a man. I'm too young for a grave.

Don't turn your back. Please come and stay.
Don't be that tomorrow who won't go away.
Today I am here. I am safe and alive.
Pull me away from tomorrow – I might not survive.

SLIPPING AWAY

The days melt together as if they were one,
With brief moments of darkness interrupting the sun.
So sad and so silent, I gaze at the sky.
Another day I am nowhere, as a cloud drifts on by.

Standing so still I feel the earth as it turns,
Wearing me down like a candle that drips as it burns.
The shadows are scary as they grow into night,
Smothering hopes that once were so bright.

The hands on the clock tick away like a knife.
As each day passes by, it cuts away at my life.
Like the flower that blooms just to wither and die,
The petals fall one by one, like the tears from each eye.

Rainbows are seldom, as the storm rages on.
I find myself drowning even after it's gone.
Gasping for air, I go under once more,
Losing the strength to make it back to the shore.

My wheels are spinning as I run, and I run.
Going nowhere too fast, as days melt into one.
As the clouds and the birds freely float by,
They laugh at me in my prison as I gaze up at their sky.

THE SEARCH

I walk through this tunnel so dark and so vast.
My mind's eye is able to look at the past.
It blinds me and traps me with all of this pain,
Like a sharp knife that stabs me again and again.

I walk through this tunnel with no end in sight.
Waiting for daybreak from this long endless night.
I feel so lonely – like a slow death from no touch.
It's just out of reach, how I need it so much.

I walk through this tunnel, wondering, where is the sky,
To offer me hope, but all I can do is cry.
Going nowhere too fast – I feel so lost.
My heart and my soul are what it has cost.

I walk through this tunnel and look back at my past.
As up ahead there's still darkness – I don't know if I'll last.
That sharp knife keeps on stabbing and bringing me pain,
Causing doubts that I'll heal and start living again.

LOVE LOST

THE DADDY WHO NEVER WAS

Daddy had to leave me. He said he had to go,
For reasons mommy told me, I was too young to know.
No more daddy's little girl, no more on daddy's knee.
Daddy said he loved me, that I could not see.

Mommy's all alone now. Often does she cry.
She tries to hide it from me and does not tell me why.
I used to write him letters. Pictures were inside.
The outside sad "To Daddy". He never has replied.

When I was very sick in bed, I called out Daddy's name.
Mommy said she'd call him, but still nobody came.
I'll always miss my Daddy, and someday I may learn,
That this man who said he loved me, never will return.

THE DADDY WHO NEVER WAS II

This boy and girl fell in love.
The boy asked – "Will you be my wife?"
To her, he vowed to be true.
"We'll have such a beautiful life."

They had 3 beautiful children,
Two boys, then me, the girl.
Still, there was something missing.
What it was, they just quite weren't sure.

One day my daddy didn't come home.
Why didn't he tell me goodbye?
But Daddy told me he loved me.
He'll be back, so I don't have to cry.

After that he hardly did see me.
When he did, he said he still cared.
But when I needed him most,
I called, but he never was there.

Oh, daddy how I wanted your love.
To hug me and give me a kiss.
To know me and watch me grow up.
There's so very much you did miss.

Your leaving left quite a scar.
Now, I'm confused about how I do feel.
I don't know if I'll every forgive you,
Because you know sometimes scars never heal.

Now after years you want back into my life.
It's too late -will you please leave me alone?
When you touch me, it feels quite cold.
Like they say -you can't go back home.

FANTASY FATHER

My real father left me some time ago.

I missed him and I needed his love.

But, when someone leaves you, they are gone for good.

So, that's how I know that he doesn't love me.

But that's okay.

Because when I sleep, I have dreams of a fantasy father.

He gives me the love I need.

He listens and cares.

I can tell him what I feel, and he tells me what he feels.

I can hug my fantasy father. He holds me so very tight.

When I have a problem, he is always there.

My fantasy father loves my mother. He treats her with warmth and respect.

He loves my brothers, too. But he cares about me the most.

I can sit on his knee and give him a kiss.

Sometimes his whiskers tickle my nose.

But I don't mind.

He tucks me in at night and tells me stories about a sweet little girl who had a father that loved her very much.

Then.... I wake up.

My fantasy father is dead. He is only alive in my dreams.

I wish that my real father was dead.

Why can't my fantasy father be my real father?

But I can't sleep my life away.

Why not? DARN IT!!

How come the only time I am happy is when I am dreaming about my fantasy father?

THE DRINKER

The drinker drinks to ease the pain.
It's what helps to keep him sane,
For this bottle he calls friend,
Is what he'll have until the end.

He puts the glass up to his lips,
And with the liquid that he sips,
He tries to fill the hole,
That goes deep into his soul.

The more that he does drink,
The less he'll have to think.
He makes himself completely numb,
So, the feelings will not come.

He stumbles as he walks,
And mumbles when he talks.
But at least he's found a way,
To make it through the day.

The drinker drinks to ease the pain,
For it's what helps to keep him sane.
And this bottle he calls friend,
Is what will lead him to his end.

FATHER'S DAY

When my father came to visit, I would always stand and watch,
As he reached into his bag and then fixed a drink of scotch.
It was only one of many he had throughout the day,
For his glass was never empty the whole time he would stay.

I would look at him with wonder, as I couldn't understand,
What was so important about what he had in his hand.
I thought that it was me that caused my dad to drink.
That was the only way I saw him. How else could I think?

His visits were quite scarce, and with that I was confused.
He just didn't seem to need me quite as much as he did booze.
His hugs, they felt like ice, and I never sat upon his knee.
He held on tighter to that bottle than he ever did to me.

Over time he did try harder, but still many years did pass,
That I sat and listened to the sound of ice clink in his glass.
This man who was my father was this stranger to my eyes.
He drowned himself in alcohol, as I drowned myself in cries.

I came to understand that he drank to ease his pain.
He was struggling for a way just to help to keep him sane.
But all this understanding will never bring the daddy back,
Or make up for the loving and affection that I lack.

The memories of my father, broken promises flowed like his scotch.
The only truth I came to know is what I endlessly would watch,
As he pulled out of his bag what was scheduled for his stay,
For his glass was never empty on visiting Father's Day.

MISSING DADDY

I sit here with this pain. My head has such an ache,
Because it won't allow my heart to feel the hurt, as it does break.
It's being torn in two by the one who was not there.
It's the absence of a daddy. He was the someone who was nowhere.

For years I did not know how I was supposed to feel,
For this man who was my father, just was not for real.
I swallowed all the pain. The anger disappeared,
But I have since discovered that they were buried under fear.

This little girl inside me now feels very sad,
And is only just beginning to speak out and get quite mad.
I missed out on something special, a daddy's tenderness and touch.
A man to care and guide me; something I needed very much.

I know that I can't ever have any of it back,
And there will never be a person to make up for what I lack.
It's just the truth about my life, that I must accept and learn,
But right now, I feel its heat as it surfaces and burns.

My head is letting go of all its pains and aches,
As it allows my lonely heart, to miss daddy as it breaks.

THE DRINKER – THE FINAL CHAPTER

The drinker drank to ease his pain,
But the drinking was in vain,
For the bottle he called friend,
Has finally led him to his end.

He tried to fill the hole,
That went deep into his soul.
But it only filled with tears,
From all he's missed throughout the years.

He lays deeply in his grave.
He no longer can be saved,
For that liquid that he sipped,
Has shortened his life's trip.

I hope he's found some peace,
So all his pain will cease.
A place where he can live,
Knowing he won't have to give.

The drinker drank to ease his pain.
It no longer was in vain.
This bottle truly was his friend,
Because it finally led him to his end.

RUSTY DOG

Rusty was my friend, but now he's very dead.
I was in the car that smashed him in the head.
He was my red, sweet puppy friend who brought me so much joy.
Now I don't know what to do without my Rusty Boy.

I'd bring him in my room, and he'd sleep up in my bed.
But now I sleep alone cause my Rusty Dog is dead.
He'd drink water from the sink and splash it on the tile.
And when he got excited, he'd wag his tail and smile.

On the night that he got killed, everyone was sad.
But they all ignored me. I think that they were mad.
I was just a little kid, confused and very scared.
I needed them to hug me to show me that they cared.

But no one ever told me that I was not to blame,
And ever since this happened, things just aren't the same.
My mother and my brothers took some time to grieve,
But when it came to missing school, my mommy made me leave.

Just because I'm only ten, doesn't mean I don't feel pain.
For Rusty was the only one who helped to keep me sane.
His fur, it was so soft. I'd pet him all the time.
Then we'd go and hide, and I'd pretend he was all mine.

For 3 years and a half he was my bestest friend,
But on one dark October night it all came to an end.
When Rusty Dog was killed, I cried and cried and cried.
It's as if we were as one and a part of me had died.

I was in the car that hit him in the head.
Rusty was my very best friend, but now he's very dead.

BOB - WINGS IN HEAVEN

I had this friend that I hardly did see.
He left without saying goodbye to me.
We laughed and played and looked at the sky.
We had loved each other and didn't have to ask why.

The last time I saw him it had been a long while.
We had parted with a hug, a kiss and a smile.
He was a good man, so young and alive.
Because of his friends he fought to survive.

Life isn't fair, the people all say,
But we must go on living each brand-new day.
There were no goodbyes, but now I can see,
The love that we shared still lives in me.

BOB – EXPLORING THE SKY

Even though we lived far apart,
He reached out with his love and touched my heart.
He was a beautiful person with much love to give.
An explorer of life with a lot more to live.

Bob was a gentle man. He was everyone's friend.
He wanted to stay, for he fought til the end.
I picture his face, my eyes fill with tears,
As I think of the love, we shared so few years.

I'll hold on to his memory and with it I'll grow,
Because he was a man, that I was so lucky to know

THE DECLINE OF DON

FROM THE LOVE OF MY LIFE,
TO MY BIGGEST HEARTBREAK

THE TREASURE

I went out for a walk in search of a warm hand
For the one who speaks the language that only lovers understand.
I longed for eyes to gaze at and for that look that warms my heart,
And for that special time and place where love can make its start.

My trip led me to you at the point where our paths crossed.
I was relieved as I remembered all the times that I'd been lost.
There was something there about you; a man who was for real.
So sensitive and caring as you allowed yourself to feel.

You've touched me very deeply. Mere words just can't express,
The warmth that does engulf me from your kiss and sweet caress.
I feel just like a flower who's buds at last a bloom,
As you nourish and support me and allow my growth its room.

Making love is like a poem with its gentle rhythm and sweet rhyme,
As our bodies join together and flow in steady time.
We share this wondrous magic, an exchanging of the soul,
And watch as we unite and create a precious whole.

Let's go for a walk and take hold of each other's hand,
And speak that special language that only lovers understand.
Let's gaze into each other's eyes and look deep into the heart,
And then we'll have this time and place, where love can make its start.

THE TRUTH

There's so much I need to tell you,
That I don't know where to start.
I've kept so many secrets,
In my head and in my heart.

They've started to build up,
So now I have this wall,
That I've put up between us.
I must somehow make it fall.

What makes this wall so sturdy,
Is that the cracks are filled with fear,
The fear that you'll abandon me,
If you don't like what you'll hear.

The fear goes very deep,
Very deep into my core.
I must fight it face-to-to face,
So, it can't hurt me anymore.

POTENTIAL

There is this sadness that I cannot describe,
For what is now missing from deep down inside.
There are all of these tears for what just can't be.
For a precious life that I'll never see.

I did the only thing that I thought I could do.
What was once a life, now is all through.
It was a difficult decision that I had to make,
As I asked a doctor for this life to take.

The pain of it all was extremely intense.
But now the guilt is so much more immense.
As a result, I feel this great big hole,
That goes very deep down into my soul.

I cry tears for the life that just cannot be,
For this precious one that I never will see.
There is such a sadness, that I can now describe,
It's about what is missing from deep down inside.

LETTING GO

Saying the words – "I love you" don't seem to be enough,
To express the way I feel through this time that's been so rough.
Your gentleness and caring as you hold me through my pain,
Is like the warmth of sunshine that brings rainbow to the rain.

I feel so safe within your arms as you softly kiss my tears.
And we grow ever closer, as we share our hopes and fears.
I know how very badly you want to take my hurt away.
And that truly touched my heart. How much I just can't say.

You are my best friend and my lover, and someday I'll be your wife.
You are that special person that I want forever in my life.
As I express how I am feeling through this time that's been so rough,
Goes way beyond the words "I love you" which just don't seem to be enough.

BEGINNINGS AND ENDINGS

Has my love come to an end?
He once was my best friend.
Although I am still his wife,
I feel so lonely in my life.

His body, it has let him down.
But I feel that I'm the one to drown.
I'm so young yet feel so old.
Instead of warmth, I feel so cold.

It is rare that I come first,
Or is it just for better or for worse?
Maybe I just feel sorry for myself,
And am not seeing all of my wealth.

I am longing for so much more,
I think it's just outside my door,
Someone else to make me feel whole,
But this thought tortures my soul.

There is this ache inside of my heart,
In considering us to part.
Do I tell him how I feel?
Or, do I continue to conceal?

Until figure this out for sure,
This torment I will endure.
Am I out or am I in?
Or is this a fight I'm too tired to win?

Is it better to be single?
To find others with whom to mingle?
For so long, I have been on my own,
For even with him, I feel so alone.

Others say I deserve to be free,
That I need some time to discover me.
There's so much about me that needs to change,
So many things that I must rearrange.

I do know now my love's come to an end,
And that he no longer is my best friend.
So, this decision to no more be a wife,
And to find out who I am in my life.

WHY I CRY

I cry because of who you became.
A pile of bones – only the name is the same.
I cry because I am wondering how,
I could have loved someone who's the way you are now.

I cry because I've spent so much of my life,
Waiting for love that I deserved as a wife,
Only to end up so tired and so all alone,
Stuck in a rut with not having grown.

I cry because it's so hard to believe,
That I have this loss that I now have to grieve.
I cry because how you only think about you,
As you use your pain to block us out of view.
I cry because I don't like how it leaves me to feel,
This sadness, this hate I can't deny that it's real.

I cry because I feel my heart start to break.
It's hard not to cry when there's such a big ache.
I cry because I know I must feel this pain.
It is the only way I will achieve any gain.

I need to learn who I am without you.
I need to learn more about all I can do.
I need to ignore how you think about me.
That's the only way I'll ever be free.
The only way that I can remain strong,
Is to remind myself that you got it all wrong.

BROKEN PROMISES

In my life the wound that I feel most deep,
Is from all the promises that men didn't keep.
This chipped away at my heart, which has left a big hole,
Where sadness has seeped down into my soul.

I never asked for much, although I knew that I should,
But I had learned when I did, it didn't do any good.
Each time I'd believe that they'd follow through,
But there'd be a letdown, just like I knew.

So, you think I'd be numb from years of the pain,
Of being disappointed time and again.
But I haven't yet learned that I can't trust the word,
That men will follow up with what I know I have heard.

I often wonder why it's so hard for these men to keep,
The promises when broken cause wounds that go deep.
It still chips away at my heart and keeps widening the hole,
Where forever the sadness seeps down into my soul.

SEARCHING

TAKING THE TIME TO FIND OUT*

I wish I could find
That peace of mind
That says I'm okay.

I'll be all right
And not get uptight.
I'll give myself time.

I need to know
A lot so I'll grow.
I have so much to learn.

I have to hear the voice,
That says I have choice
To be what I want.

Me: a person.

*Taking the Time To Find Out, from the album –
"Let it Flow" by Dave Mason*

THE STRUGGLE, THE SEARCH FOR ME

Twenty-eight years ago, I was born, and on that day the world had forever changed because I was in it.

It was at that time that I began my search, or should I say, my struggle to find my purpose for being, to discover why it was that this person, me, was created.

After all of this time, I am no closer to the answer.

This person, me, feels like this person, not me.

I float around like a cloud with nowhere to go, just taking up space in the sky.

There is this woman part of me, that has not been discovered, or appreciated by the man part of a man.

Or, maybe, I haven't appreciated the woman part of me enough for it to be noticeable to the man part of them.

This feeling of non-being isn't a feeling of wanting to die, or wishing I was never born, it's a feeling of frustration. This body and this brain and all of the existence within it, wants to be as one, to work together to do something for this world.

This person, me, wants to be happy, has a right to be happy just for the right of being, just as every person deserves and has a right to happiness.

In my search, struggle, I seem to forget this. If I fail at any one of my many attempts of discovery, or if I don't spend every waking moment trying to achieve of the goals that I have set for myself, I punish myself. I feel guilty and deny myself pleasures. I tell myself that I don't deserve any happiness.

Like the floating cloud, I feel so alone, although I see other clouds out there probably feeling much the same way.

I reach out and touch others sometimes; my friends help me try and make it through,

They are wonderful, as they share their experiences of non-personness. But being there isn't always enough, because when it comes right down to it, we are only left with ourselves. We are all alone together in our discovery.

I am scared of being just the cloud that floats. I want to be the cloud that rains down and becomes part of the earth, to contribute something to this world.

This person, not me wants to feel like the person me that it deserves to feel like.

When I begin to fee like a person, I will be happy, and I know my life will have purpose, and the woman part of me will reveal itself to me, and then it will become evident to the men persons out there.

Twenty-eight years ago, I was born, and on that day the world had forever changed because of it.

I am no closer to the answer of how it is I will have an effect, but maybe this is the way of telling me that just my being here is a gift in itself.

Be happy just being. I don't have to earn the happiness.

No matter what I do or don't do, I am contributing wonderful things, because I am the best and only me that there is.

I may never find an answer, for my purpose is the struggle…the search.

BEING ME

Who can really say whether how I cope is wrong or right.
I can only do my best to win my endless fight.
There are things I need to work on, and things I should or should not do.
But I can still only be myself as I struggle to get through.
When you give advice, I know that you do care.
But what I really need is for you to just be there.
I'll keep coming back, because it's still a safer place,
For me to share my thoughts and feelings, face to face to face.
So, as we continue with our struggles, and each do our best to cope,
There is no right or wrong way, as long as we have hope.

GROWING AWAY

I said goodbye, and she started to cry.
She was losing her baby.

But she has to know that I have to grow.
I'm still her baby.

I hope she's okay being alone this way.
How she misses her baby.

I'm learning to see how to be me.
Gosh, how I miss my mother.

AHEAD TO THE PAST

I have finally decided to move back to my home.
Seven years that I have been gone.
I need to figure things out, to make a fresh start,
And to find out where I belong.

Leaving memories and friends, it's going to be hard.
There were good times mixed in with the bad.
I learned a lot about life, other people, myself.
I grew up here, I know I'll be sad.

Is this the best thing? I don't really know.
But here, I'm just spinning my wheels.
I'm taking two giant steps backward to try and get me ahead.
So uncomfortable all of this feels.

Will I get support from the loved ones back home?
Or will I get pulled back under their spell?
Protected and coddled and told what to do.
Here or there, the choice seems to be hell.

The choice that I make, if it's right or it's wrong.
Time will tell me what I need to know.
My eyes are wide open as I take it one day at a time.
More I'll learn, more I'll love, more I'll grow.

HEALING AND GROWTH

A FAMILIAR JOURNEY
(FOR EILEEN)

I tell my friends my problems,
I know that they listen and care.
They say that they know how I'm feeling.
But how can they, they weren't ever there.

When we talked things seemed to be different.
I had said those same words once before.
I knew then and there you were special.
We had walked that same rocky shore.

I am sometimes so sad and so lonely.
You said you were once that way too.
Waiting so long for love to come by,
Loneliness was all that you knew.

Now there's a love in your life.
And I am still looking for mine.
You say I should not give up hope,
For I am young and have plenty of time.

I am really glad we are friends.
And I know that your feelings are true.
I know that you do understand me.
Because you were once at that place too.

A WELCOME REST

There's this pounding in her head,
And ringing in her ears.
The pain is so intense,
It's bringing her to tears.

The ringing is getting louder.
The pounding will not stop.
It's hurting her so much,
I think she's going to drop.

She can't take it any longer,
The tears fall from her eyes.
Doesn't anybody hear her?
As she can't hold back her cries.

She hears somebody knocking.
She asks out loud, "Who's there?"
A voice answers back – "A friend.
I am someone who does care."

The ringing has died down.
The pounding, it has ceased.
The pressures of her life,
All have been released.

Someone felt her pain,
Cause they had been there once before.
The hurt that she was having,
Will be gone forever more.

BREAKING OUT

I stood at the mirror and looked at me,
And saw only things that I wanted to see.
That piece of glass hanging on the wall,
Reflected my life. It had said it all.
It's not alive, so how can it know,
The places I've been to or where I will go?

I stood at the mirror and looked at me.
A girl in a shell was all I could see.
I turned away for a moment and then tried hard to hide,
From the truth and the feelings that lay burning inside.
I had to look – it was calling me back.
It was trying to tell me of the love that I lack.

I stood at the mirror and looked at me.
I saw only the things that I wanted to see.
I noticed the glass was starting to fall.
That darned old mirror was a know-it-all.
We lay there in pieces, that mirror and me.
The shell's finally broken -at last I am free.

LOOK WHO I'VE FOUND

I met this stranger at the beach.

At first, I thought I knew him.

But I changed my mind when I saw him.

The color of his hair, the shape of his face.

The resemblance is amazing, but everybody has a double.

He seemed at peace with himself.

He didn't care that his pants were all wet.

It was as if it was the first time, he was ever part of nature.

He stood on a rock and just looked out to the sea,

And listened to the sound of the waves, as if they were telling him the answers to the problems in his life.

I think that what it was trying to tell him, was that he was meant to be here,

That everything, and everyone had some reason for being on this earth.

I looked again and realized that I knew him after all.

Who I saw, was me, becoming a person.

COMING UP FOR AIR

I've probably wasted so many years,
Trying to swim in my pool of tears.
I had been convinced for such a long time,
That I was helpless and couldn't use my own mind.

Loneliness was like a ride that just wouldn't stop.
It sometimes got too fast, that I felt ready to drop.
There were friends and lovers that I wanted so bad,
But the courage to get them was not too be had.

I built a wall that was so strong and so tall.
I saw people try but they could not make it fall.
I was protecting myself from what causes pain.
I was safe, and alive, but crying in vain.

What is it that scared me? Why did I hide?
As I continued to drown in these tears that I cried.
Time was running short as I was gasping for breath.
I must take a risk, for it's better than death.

I finally found out after all of this time,
That I wasn't helpless and that I had a bright mind.
So, I stopped fighting myself and looked all around.
I climbed over the wall and put both feet on the ground.

I found out there were people who really do care,
Who had laughter and friendship and loving to share.
I had been missing a lot from all of these fears,
That were foolish as I was trying to swim in my tears.

THE FIRST STEP

I looked outside and saw a blue, blue sky.
Not a cloud in sight. Only birds flying high.
How lucky they are to be so free.
They go everywhere they want, even out to the sea.

I see myself so unlike the bird,
So afraid to be free. I don't say a word.
My world is the sky I will not explore.
I won't go anywhere I haven't been to before.

Those beautiful creatures how foolish they are.
They don't think about the danger of going too far.
It is I who's the fool who won't take the flight,
Of discovering things that are way beyond sight.

The sun might scorch their wings. The birds don't really care.
They keep flying higher and farther to see what's out there.
If I take the step, I might trip and fall.
But if I don't pick up my feet, I'll go nowhere at all.

The winged beasts are so very alive.
They have so much beauty yet know how to survive.
I learn a valuable lesson when I look at the sky.
That in order to grow, I must first learn to fly.

CATHARSIS

Sometimes I have a need to be alone with all my pain,
And let go of all the tears like the sky lets go of rain.
The air becomes quite clear, and life begins anew.
The buds again start blooming, being fed by drops of dew.

Sometimes a storm starts raging – sometimes it's just a shower.
But, when the sky does clear, there remains a precious flower.
Over time I do start growing, as I give my petals to the wind.
Baring all my soul, and risking pain again.

The sky goes through its seasons of laughter and of tears,
A cycle it's endured for a countless span of years.
Like the sky I have my moments filled with lots of pain.
But I know that magic trick the sun plays on the rain.

I listen to the pain, as the tears flow from my eyes.
I feel the joy of rain as the clouds release their cries.
The hurt that eats me up inside, I just have to let it go,
For it's what showers me with strength, that in turn helps me to grow.

THE KEYHOLDER
(FOR RICHARD)

You noticed I seemed to be trapped in a cell,
So, you tried to release me from my prison of hell.
The bars I'd put up to avoid getting too close,
But, at the very same time, it's what I needed the most.

I have handcuffed myself to a life filled with fear.
I cross off days on the wall as I waste yet one more year.
This life of confusion. It must be rearranged.
My past and my present; the scene has not changed.

My body told you a story, that you read like a book.
You held up a mirror and forced me to look.
It showed tales of struggles on a face lined in pain,
So tired from fighting, as I work hard to keep sane.

You say I look so young, yet I feel very old.
My walls block out the sun, as I shiver with cold.
There's a lump in my throat, as tears well up in my eyes.
It takes all of my strength to hold back the cries.

The hours pass by quickly, as we talked, and we shared.
And by the end of the night, we knew how much each other cared.
As we hugged very tightly, I didn't want it to end.
I treasured that moment because I had discovered a friend.

A BREAK IN THE CLOUDS
(FOR RICHARD)

Each time we'd get near, I would put up a wall, when it was friendship that I needed the most.

I would think about something that I wanted to share, but I was just too afraid to get close.

We would look at each other for days upon end, never quite knowing what we should say.

But I noticed this change when I went over to see you and said that I was moving away.

That night when we talked, you really caught me off guard, so quickly you cracked through my shell.

Discovering things that I tried to keep hidden, away with me in my cell.

You would run up against bars that I'd put up in defense, for fear you'd uncover my pain.

But you worked your way through them, and got at the truth, that I had locked up so tight in my brain.

You did a lot of the talking, but I still felt relief, as the picture became very clear.

So many things that I needed to say, and even more that I needed to hear.

When you hugged me so tight, it went straight to my heart and it showed me how much you do care.

But I'll be far away now, and when I reach out, I'll miss that you won't be there.

There was so little time for us to be friends, but it's a friendship that I will hold dear.

How can I forget someone, who in such a short time, helped me to let go of my fear.

I'm only mad at myself, all the time I did waste, sitting alone in my room.

While not far away from my door, was this bright ray of sun, waiting to shine through my gloom.

WISDOM OF THE WAVES

The crashing of the waves takes away my thoughts of sadness and carries them out to sea.

This wonder of nature is temporarily struggling to help me feel free.

With such intensity, they pound the rocks and shore, attempting to kill my pain so I would feel it never more.

Fail as they will, for my burdens only strengthen and resist as time goes on.

That is really okay, because, at least for one day, I will be at peace.

The sounds of the sea drown out my despair and doubt.

Waves break high and low, not sure of where they should go.

Sometimes I want to jump in and swim and swim and swim away from it all, or maybe keep my head under and cut off every breath.

I would no longer suffer, but the answer is not death.

The ocean, give me strength to carry on, for your relief, is so short.

The power and force help put me back on course.

I've already told you, don't attempt to kill what cannot die. So endlessly you try and try.

Give to me your persistence and your fight and your gentle stillness when you have found out what is right.

So much potential, so many choices.

I get it…all along that's what you've been trying to tell me.

WHAT'S MISSING

In my life right now what's missing
Is someone who'll really listen.
As equals we would share,
To each other we'd show we care.
Touching bodies, touching minds
In search of answers, we must find.
So, if you have an ear, please listen.
You may be just what I've been missing.

DIRECTIONS

Thinking that there is only one path I can take,
Is where I have made my biggest mistake.
My life is a circle, and from the center I see,
The many roads I must take that all lead back to me.

Each one has 3 lanes – work, love and play.
Keeping both feet in each one, I must do every day.
After time I grow weary, as I near this path's end.
But soon a new view, and then on the trail once again.

One constant lover would help narrow my road.
Walking through life together, we could lighten the load.
The trip up ahead still might be rough,
But we'll have each other to lean on when the going gets tough.

Thinking that there is only one path I can take,
I am no longer making that fatal mistake.
Inside this circle, with my love, I can see,
The many roads we must take that all lead back to we.

OPENING UP

I will never see the sunrise until I look out over the mountains.

I will never see the moon and the stars until I gaze up at the sky.

I will never grow, until I reach for what is just beyond sight and sound, smell and touch.

LIVING IN THE PAST

I used to write of all my pain as I struggled to survive.
But all that I accomplished was to keep the pain alive.
I thought that it would help me by writing it all down.
But all I'd get were tears – enough to make me drown.

This pain can be of value in helping me to grow.
But it will not help me, until I let it go.
I cannot move forward by living in the past.
And writing all these words down takes me nowhere fast.

Now I'll have to write of joy and love and hope.
The words will be of growing, and not just how to cope.
They will be poems for the future, and how I am right now.
No more whys and what ifs. All I'll ask is how?

I will not forget those days that have gone by.
But I must keep them in the past where they can't make me cry.
No more using words as a place for me to hide.
Instead, they'll be a way to find what's deep inside.

BEING THERE
(FOR BRAD)

I was down so very low, almost giving up the fight.
Someone heard my silent screams and pulled me up into the light.
He was here to help me, he said he was my friend.
He would see me make it through. He had an ear to lend.

Somehow he knew I was in pain, and that I was fighting back the tears.
For he had also suffered from an avalanche of fears.
He said that there were others who spoke these things out loud.
I would not be alone – he introduced me to this crowd.

THE MYSTERY TRIP

Every morning when I wake up, I don't know what's in store.
It's a trip to the unknown when I step outside my door.
For at night when I am sleeping, secret forces plan my day.
Plotting all my thoughts and moves and what I'm going to say.

Somedays it is quite peaceful, like being in a dream.
But sometimes it is a nightmare where no one hears me scream.
I always am relieved when I survive another fight,
And then I can rest and watch the dark as it overtakes the light.

Then I think about these forces. There's a great deal that they know,
As they're providing me with challenges, for that's the only way I'll grow.
So, every morning when I wake up and wonder what's in store,
It's one more trip to the unknown that waits outside my door.

HEALING

The little child has been born.
From her world of silence, she's been torn.
To find a place where she can feel,
And where she can share, and she can heal.
She has learned that she can cope,
For she takes with her strength and hope.

SETTING LIMITS

I always aim to please and do what I am told,
And find it very hard to stand up and be so bold.
I always do forget that I do have a choice,
To speak up for myself and use God's gift of my voice.

THE CLEARING

I looked out the window and started to smile,
For I'd discovered the beauty that had been lost for a while.
I feel fulfilled, well I'm at least on my way.
My outlook is bright, as I live life day by day.

I reflect on my past and face all the pain.
This is what I must do to start living again.
The's sun's dried up the rain. The sky's finally clear.
And now I can see that hope is once again near.

I no longer dread all the clouds nor the darkness of night.
For the sun always comes back to show me the light.
The room in my heart has found the help from above,
For the sky has reached down and touched it with love.

I stare out the window and continue to smile,
For I still see the beauty that's been here all the while.
My outlook is still bright, and I know I'm on my way,
And that I'll be fulfilled if I just live life day by day.

CUTTING THE CORD

The time has finally come, and now at last I know,
What it's going to take to really help me grow.
I have to make a break, and be free from family ties,
And see this great big world by way of my own eyes.

I know that it is hard, but for my own sake,
That I need to learn and grow and make my own mistakes.
There are many brand-new shores that I have yet to see,
Before I can discover the truth inside of me.

Until now this big, wide world has been somewhat like a book,
That I have not yet opened, for I've been too scared to look.
And when I do need help, I can just reach out my hand,
Because I know I'm not alone. I have friends who understand.

So much the need for freedom to explore the big, blue sky,
Just like an awkward bird who is learning how to fly.
As I said, I know it's hard, but I can learn and grow,
And when I learn to love myself, I finally will let go.

ONE DAY SOMEONE IS GOING TO HUG YOU SO TIGHT THAT ALL OF YOUR BROKEN PIECES WILL STICK BACK TOGETHER
(FOR DAVID)

This time that you did hug me, with caring touch from you, dear friend,
It was the glue I needed to help my broken pieces mend.
I am glad you knew I needed to be held so very tight,
Something so long elusive, happened on this night.

The warmth of your sweet breath, your sweet and gentle touch.
I never thought human contact could ever mean so much.
Such soothing words you whispered, so softly in my ear.
Words I only could imagine, and never thought I'd hear.

You helped wrap my arms around you, into your shoulder I did melt.
Feeling all these painful feelings that I had long since felt.
This was the first time that I ever, through all my lonely years,
Was able to let someone support me through my tears.

Other times have followed, which have helped me feel alive.
Saying things and touching me and helping me to thrive.
It is really about connection of the mind, and heart and soul.
Being more than just our bodies, we are uniting as a whole.

This time that you did hug me, my broken pieces, they did mend,
With glue that only comes from the caring touch of a dear friend.
Thank you for just knowing that is what I needed on this night.
Often elusive, yet so simple to have someone hold me oh so tight.

A HEALING TOUCH
(FOR ANDY)

When I first read your sweet gentle words,
It started bringing tears to each eye,
For I've had so much pain, from being alone,
Yet I have never let myself cry.

There's this hole that goes deep in my heart,
From the absence of a healing touch,
Which is still in my sight, yet just out of reach.
Oh, how I need it so very much.

Being held tightly in somebody's arms,
So desperately I have craved.
I keep waiting for someone, to finally come by,
To hold me and help me be saved.

But these occasions have ended up being,
So too few and far between.
It makes me feel sad, and very alone,
That I continue not to be seen.

As I keep reading your sweet gentle words,
It is still bringing tears to each eye.
But you will be with me to help ease my pain.
Your healing touch will allow me to cry.

A HELPING HAND

Friends are so important; without them we would die.
We need them to help us make it through, or at least to just get by.
We all thrive on each other, why else would there be this crowd.
But sometimes to let us know you're there, is by yelling right out loud.

I am here to help you. I want to be your friend.
I want to see you make it through, I have an ear to lend.
I know I don't hear every cry of all who are in pain.
But, I'd like to bring to just one man the sun to dry his rain.

I've been down before, almost giving up the fight.
Someone heard my silent screams and pulled me up into the light.
It's alright to need another, that's why we all are here.
But if you don't speak up, I'll understand, I'll hear you loud and clear.

www.ingramcontent.com/pod-product-compliance
Lightning Source LLC
LaVergne TN
LVHW041610070526
838199LV00052B/3074